REAL ESTATE 101

A Guide for Military Personnel

DAVID L. RUFFIN

Copyright © 2020 David L. Ruffin.

All rights reserved. No part of this book may be reproduced, stored, or transmitted by any means—whether auditory, graphic, mechanical, or electronic—without written permission of the author, except in the case of brief excerpts used in critical articles and reviews. Unauthorized reproduction of any part of this work is illegal and is punishable by law.

ISBN: 978-1-7167-0228-0 (sc)
ISBN: 978-1-7169-3295-3 (e)

Library of Congress Control Number: 2020909398

Because of the dynamic nature of the Internet, any web addresses or links contained in this book may have changed since publication and may no longer be valid. The views expressed in this work are solely those of the author and do not necessarily reflect the views of the publisher, and the publisher hereby disclaims any responsibility for them.

Any people depicted in stock imagery provided by Getty Images are models, and such images are being used for illustrative purposes only. Certain stock imagery © Getty Images.

Lulu Publishing Services rev. date: 07/30/2020

Introduction

AT THE TIME OF THIS writing, the United States is experiencing very unique and volatile financial markets associated with the economic turmoil created by the COVID-19 virus, including those related to housing and mortgage investments. I believe this to be a temporary condition and fully expect the markets to return to a more stable order consistent with the past decade (2010 – 2020). Because of this, I have confidence in the underlying principles discussed in this book and believe them to be applicable in the future.

Welcome to the world of real estate! In some fashion or another I have been involved in real estate for over thirty years, either as an owner, investor, "flipper", or a broker. I know of no other industry that is so diverse, offering any number of opportunities to invest and receive both the tax benefits and returns that many real estate investments do. First and foremost, real estate fills a basic need – shelter! An obvious fact is that you (and your family) need a place to live. As a military member, you will likely be searching for a home every three or four years, and you will need a comfortable, enjoyable, safe place to live. Note that I did not mention that you need to find the perfect home.

For most of you this home is not your dream retirement home. *You need to find the home that will be the most marketable, for either sale or rent, to the largest segment of the population, three to four years down the road.* I have made many mistakes over my thirty years of real estate, but fortunately none of them were horrible mistakes. A perfect example from my early real estate life was that even though I didn't need much for my first home (I was single with a dog), the majority of prospective buyers or renters did have a larger family and needed more space. My 1400 sq ft, 3 bed,

1 ½ bath home was not very marketable to the couple with two young kids. Likewise, since I was single, I paid little attention to school districts, and that was a big mistake. Probably the number one consideration for most young families (for either purchase or renting) is ensuring their kids are going to a good school. It doesn't have to be the very top school, but it sure cannot be in the bottom tier of schools.

As you go through the home search process, please keep in mind the end-objective for this home you are considering buying; will it be for resale or to rent as an investment property. I don't want to use the term "generic", but you should be tailoring your search for the 1700 – 2200 sq ft home with three bedrooms and an office or four bedrooms, minimum two car garage, and probably a fenced back yard for kids or pets. Each one of these home purchases you make throughout your career will be a stepping stone to eventually buying or building your dream retirement home when that day arrives! Congratulations again on taking the first step into the fantastic world of real estate.

1

Buy vs. Rent

AS ACTIVE-DUTY MILITARY, ONE OF the biggest real estate questions that you will likely face several times throughout your career is whether to rent a place to live or to purchase a home. For most of the past couple decades, I've been on the fence as far as this question is concerned. However, several things have happened in the last decade that have led me to be a little more bullish toward buying.

First and foremost, mortgage rates are extremely low. Simply put, today your buying power is much higher than it was ten or fifteen years ago. My first home, purchased in 1996, was a little, $94,000, new construction home in Abilene, Texas. At the time, I got an 8 percent mortgage (and I was fortunate to get it that low), and my total monthly payment, including taxes and insurance, was about $860 per month. That same $860 monthly payment today at a 3.5 percent mortgage rate can buy you a $160,000 home. Same $860 a month, but you're able to purchase so much more.

Another reason I tend to lean toward buying today is that nationwide, rents have increased substantially over the last ten years. When the real estate bubble crashed back in 2007, a large number of people who previously owned a home were forced to rent. As with all supply and demand, as demand increases, so do the associated prices. With the increase in people wanting—or having—to rent, rental rates increased. Additionally, military towns and communities have always been high rental areas; property owners in those communities know that many military members do not make large salaries, will only be there for about three years, and will most likely just want to rent. Once again, the large demand for rental properties drives the rent prices higher.

With these higher rental rates, you will want to do a cost comparison between renting and buying. Let's look at an example in Enid, Oklahoma. One of the typical rental properties (three bed, two bath, 1,700 sq. ft., nicely appointed) rents at $1,500 per month. That same home would sell for about $180,000, which would approximate a monthly mortgage payment of about $1,000 (obviously dependent on credit score, interest rate, and so on). That's a $500 monthly savings by owning the home versus renting. That's $6,000 a year, $18,000 over the three-year assignment period, and if you add in the approximate $2,000 a year in tax benefits, that's a $24,000 difference in your financial position by owning rather than renting. Now not all markets will have that high of a disparity between rental rates and mortgage payments, but even a $200 per month difference results in an approximate $13,000 difference in your financial position over a three-year period. That's substantial. Even if the rental rates and mortgage payments were equal, you would still be realizing the $2,000/year tax benefit and be building equity in the property.

Notes

2

Real Estate as an Investment

UP TO THIS POINT IN many people's lives, housing expenses have been viewed as just that—an expense. That needs to change. From this point on, you should view your house as an investment. Not only is it truly an investment, it will probably outperform what you traditionally view as your investments, such as your stocks, bonds, and mutual funds.

When discussing real estate with folks, I hear these common statements: "When I sell my house, I'd like to make $X," or, "I need to fix this and update that so I can make a profit when I sell my house." In some instances, those could be valid approaches. However, after living all across this country, big cities, small towns, good economies, and bad, it has become obvious to me that you make money on a home purchase when you buy it properly. When I say *properly*, I mean you buy the right house in the right neighborhood for the right price. That's why we do what we do here with our network of agents. If our clients get matched with a good, honest, reputable agent, their likelihood of buying a home properly increases dramatically. Their risk is reduced dramatically. And three or four years later, when it's time to sell their home, their stress is significantly less because, more likely than not, they have a little room to play with financially.

Now, other than death and taxes, there are no guarantees in life, and that is absolutely true with real estate. Yet it also remains true that there is no investment vehicle out there that can give you the leverage for your money like real estate can.

Let's look at an example to truly see the benefits of real estate as an investment. Imagine that you have $20,000 to invest. Obviously you have a lot of options as to where to invest it. For the purpose of this example, let's say you decide to buy $20,000 worth of AT&T stock ("T" on NYSE, excellent stock, global company, well diversified, and approximately a 7 percent dividend). Tomorrow you will actually own $20,000 worth of stock. Now let's say it has a strong year, earning 10 percent in value. At the end of the year, what do you have? You have $22,000 worth of stock, not considering any dividend reinvestment. Your investment of $20,000 has made you $2,000 in profit if you were to sell.

What if you were to invest your $20,000 in real estate? How much real estate could you buy? With a typical conventional loan for a primary residence, you are usually required to put 5 percent down (or 3 percent for first-time homebuyers[1]). That means for a $20,000 down payment, you could purchase a $400,000 home. Now let's say it does average to below average in appreciation and only appreciates 2 percent for the year. Your home's value would be $408,000—an $8,000 increase in value.

Comparing the two options, your average to below average real estate investment made four times what the very strong stock investment made. The reason for this is simple—leverage. Your ability to *leverage* your money when investing in real estate is the reason that real estate has created more millionaires in this country than any other investment vehicle. You are buying a $400,000 asset with only $20,000 of your capital. And we haven't even begun to talk about the tax benefits, depreciation, investment property opportunities, or any of the other benefits of owning real estate. So yes, we are obviously very pro real estate. Every day

---

[1] A first-time homebuyer is someone who has never owned a home before or has not owned a home in the last three years. Most lenders can offer this, but some may not. Please check with your lender, and be aware there may be pricing and interest rate implications when doing less than 5 percent.

people are fretting over the horrible real estate markets around the country, and in some cases, those folks are justified. It is likely they paid too much for their home when they bought it, or it was in a very volatile area and they are upside down; that is, they owe more on the property than it is worth. When we look at the real estate markets, we see tremendous opportunities. In almost all areas prices have dropped dramatically, and interest rates are as low as you will probably ever see again in your life. That doesn't mean you should rush out and buy a $400K condo in South Beach or Las Vegas. It means you should talk with one of our network agents, who are experts in the local real estate market. Explain to them what you're looking for, what you would like to achieve with your home purchase, and let them do the legwork in helping you find a quality home that your family can live in comfortably with less risk and stress.

Notes

3

The Real Estate Crash

THERE WERE MANY FACTORS CONTRIBUTING to the fall in the real estate market. The crash didn't happen immediately; it actually occurred over approximately three to four years. In 2006 subprime mortgages (those made to customers with less-than-perfect credit) made up nearly 20 percent of the market. During the Clinton presidency (1993–2001), his administration was essentially forcing banks to lend to low-credit individuals or face large fines. Individuals were getting no-doc loans, basically not having to prove their creditworthiness through pay statements, tax returns, or bank balances. Many of these subprime mortgages were then packaged together and underwritten by major banks and insurance companies (like AIG) and resold on secondary markets as investment vehicles. The result was a huge influx of new home buyers who really shouldn't have been buying because of their credit and/or financial positions, or home buyers who were purchasing much more expensive homes than they should have. As owners began defaulting and getting foreclosed on, the whole scenario began to unravel.

Many today still worry about whether the real estate and housing market could see a similar crash to that of 2006–2009. I think this is unlikely, but you absolutely cannot predict the future. As a result of the crash in real estate, several safeguards were put in place to prevent this from happening again. First, no-doc loans are not done anymore. One of the least enjoyable steps of buying a home today is the small mountain of paperwork your lender will likely require you to send to them. Mortgage credit and underwriting standards are at an all-time high. Second, the appraisal process also has newer, more stringent guidelines on how home values are determined, and the appraisers are required to show documentation/proof on how they derived their valuations, thus greatly reducing the probability of artificially inflating property values.

Additionally, the foundation underlying the housing market is much stronger today than during the 2006–2009 crash. The majority of the country is seeing a rise in median family incomes and lower interest rates nationwide. The average payment-to-income ratio is just over 20 percent, compared to nearly 35 percent from 2000 to 2007. Broken down, this simply means that housing is more affordable today in most parts of the country, though there are still some areas, like coastal California, New York, and Washington DC that are well above that average and probably always will be. The US economy is experiencing a much higher participation in the workforce, and hourly earnings are increasing as well. This results in a greater number of well-qualified home buyers to go along with a reduced number of home inventories. These are two additional characteristics that were not present a decade ago.

Although recent news headlines may be reminiscent of the bubble era, the fundamental conditions that led to the crash have diminished. The real estate market today has a stronger foundation than it did in 2006, thanks to more a disciplined and conservative credit underwriting of debt and a market that is much healthier than it has been at any point during the past decade.

Notes

4

Tax Benefits of Home Ownership[2]

I WANTED TO PASS ON some tax ideas and topics for all to consider. I recently ran across some excellent info from FoxBusiness.com, but I remind everyone to stay abreast on the latest tax news. New administrations and Congresses are constantly changing the tax structure in this country, and unless you're a working CPA, you're probably not completely up to speed on the latest changes. These can have significant impact on your real estate, both primary residences and investment properties.

There are many benefits and rewards of owning a home as either your primary residence or as an investment. But many folks overlook the fact that owning a home could mean you qualify for tax breaks. Although you'll likely need to itemize your taxes in order to take advantage of these deductions, the benefits may far outweigh the complications of the tax forms.

Following are some of the tax breaks and areas you'll want to look at.

Mortgage Interest Paid at Settlement

Your closing statement should list your home mortgage interest. On a mortgage of up to $1 million, you can deduct the interest that you pay at settlement if you itemize your deductions on Schedule

---

[2] Tax laws and codes are constantly changing and have likely changed since the time of writing. You should always check on current tax conditions with a CPA or tax professional.

A (Form 1040). This amount should be included in the mortgage interest statement provided by your lender.

Points

If you paid points on your mortgage, these fees are included on the income tax deductions list and can be deducted as long as they are associated with the purchase of a home. If you refinanced your home, these points are still deductible, but it must be done over the life of the mortgage.

Property Taxes

You can deduct your state and local property taxes as long as they are based on the assessed value of the real property. If your money is being held in escrow for the purpose of paying property taxes, you cannot claim this deduction until the money is actually taken out of escrow and paid. Check your Form 1098 for the amount you may deduct.

Selling Costs

If you sold a home in the past year, you may be able to reduce your income tax by the amount of your selling costs. These costs can include things such as repairs, title insurance, advertising expenses, and broker's fees. The IRS only allows the deduction of repair costs associated with selling if the repairs were made within ninety days of the sale. It's also crucial that the repairs were made with the intent of improving your home's marketability. Selling costs are deducted from your gain on the sale.

Home Office

If you use a portion of your home exclusively for the purpose of an office for your small business, you may be able to claim a deduction on your taxes for costs related to insurance, repairs, and depreciation. You may only claim this deduction if the space within your home is used exclusively and regularly as either your principal place of business or a place where you meet and deal with customers or patients. You may also be able to take advantage of this deduction if a portion of your home routinely is used for storing items (product samples, inventory, and so on) used in your business.

Mortgage Insurance Premiums

You may be able to deduct the premiums paid for private mortgage insurance for your principal residence and for a non-rental second home. The deduction begins to phase out once your adjusted gross income reaches $100,000 ($50,000 for married filing separately). In general, you can deduct the premiums paid for the current tax year only.

Home Improvement Loan Interest

If you've taken out a loan to make improvements on your home, the interest may be deductible. The loans must be for capital improvements to your home, meaning the improvement must increase your home's value, adapt it to new uses, or extend its life. New carpeting or painting are not considered capital improvements, while adding a garage, installing a water heater, or building a deck are all examples of capital improvements.

Construction Loan Interest

If you take out a construction loan to build a home, you may qualify to deduct the interest. The IRS only allows a deduction for mortgage interest if the loan relates to a qualified home, which means it must either be your principal residence or a vacation home that you will use for personal purposes. You can only use this deduction for the first twenty-four months of the loan, even if the actual construction takes longer.

We recommend you consult the IRS website for information concerning deductions and credits, and consider meeting with a tax professional to ensure you're not missing any deductions for which you're eligible.

Capital Gains Tax[3]

If you were to sell your non-real estate investment, you will have to pay capital gains tax, which will vary depending on the duration that you owned the investment; it could be as high as 24 percent or 32 percent. By contrast, with a real estate investment, you will likely either not have to pay capital gains or will be able to defer any tax payments for quite a while (you should definitely speak with a CPA or tax professional). Many homeowners become real estate investors when they move. They keep the house that was formerly their primary residence and rent it out as an investment property. That's when the tax benefits really kick in.

Once the home becomes an investment property, nearly everything becomes an expense. The fire policy insurance premiums, property manager fees, property repairs and upgrades are all expenses that you will deduct from your rent collected to determine your net profit, and thus your taxable income. But it doesn't stop there. Even if you end up showing a net profit, your CPA can now depreciate the asset—even though in actuality your home probably appreciates—thus showing a loss and reducing the amount of your taxable income. Once you have a property that you use as an investment property, I highly recommend spending the $300 to $500 to hire a CPA to do your taxes. It is money very well spent, and it is also tax deductible.

---

[3] Tax laws and codes are constantly changing and have likely changed since the time of writing. You should always check on current tax conditions with a CPA or tax professional.

Capital Gains Tax

Capital gains tax is paid on profits or gains from selling capital assets, property, and possessions. If you sell your home for more than what you paid (minus fees, closing costs, and so on), you made a profit or gain on the asset and would have to pay the capital gains tax. If you sell the asset in one year or less, you would pay short-term capital gains; more than one year, you would pay long-term capital gains. However, under the new Tax Cuts and Jobs Act (as of 2018), the rules for the capital gains on real estate have changed somewhat.

Short-Term Capital Gains Tax Brackets			
Tax Bracket/Rate	Single	Married Filing Jointly	Head of Household
10%	$0–$9,700	$0–$19,400	$0–$13,850
12%	$9,701–$39,475	$19,401–$78,950	$13,851–$52,850
22%	$39,476–$84,200	$78,951–$168,400	$52,851–$84,200
24%	$84,201–$160,725	$168,401–$321,450	$84,201–$160,700
32%	$160,726–$204,100	$321,451–$408,200	$160,701–$204,100
35%	$204,101–$510,300	$408,201–$612,350	$204,101–$510,300
37%	$510,301+	$612,351+	$510,301+

As a comparison, long-term capital gains rates are substantially lower.

Long-Term Capital Gains Tax Brackets			
Tax Bracket/Rate	Single	Married Filing Jointly	Head of Household
0%	$0–$39,375	$0–$78,750	$0–$52,750
15%	$39,376–$434,550	$78,751–$488,850	$52,751–$461,700
20%	$434,551+	$488,851+	$461,701+

Tax Exemption for Primary Residence

In contrast to stocks, bonds, mutual funds, and other financial investments, profits from the sale of your home might exempt you from tax on capital gains entirely. Under IRS rules, each person receives a $250,000 tax-free exemption on capital gains from a primary residence regardless of how much the person earns. Until 1988, this exemption was more of a capital gains deferral or rollover that accumulated over the years. Now you can exclude this capital gain from your income permanently as long as certain provisions and requirements apply, or partial exemption under certain circumstances.

The home must be your primary residence.

You must have owned the home for at least two years.

You must have lived in the home for at least two of the past five years.

You cannot have taken this exclusion in the past two years.

Notes

5

Real Estate Agents and Professionals (Arguably the most important chapter)

PROBABLY THE SINGLE BEST THING you, as a buyer, can do is work with an honest, top-notch real estate agent who cares more about your six-figure investment and financial well-being than their commission check. Sound easy? Think again.

I want to show a little restraint here and not cast dispersions across an entire industry. But in good faith and conscience, I'm also going to tell you the unvarnished truth as to what I've seen over the last thirty years. Those honest, top-notch real estate agents are extremely hard to find. Don't get me wrong: The overwhelming majority of them are extremely nice and friendly, but that doesn't make them good real estate agents. A good agent is going to go over and above the minimum required of an agent and do the extra work to ensure that you do not overpay for a property, even at the expense of their own commissions. Considering that the real estate world is extremely competitive—and for many, commissions are few and far between—the desire to make that next check at any expense can be very strong. My heart goes out to all of the agents struggling to make a living, and I wish them all the best. But I absolutely cannot recommend any of them to our military clients because buying a home properly, at or below market value, is absolutely critical to a member of the military! Like it or not, you will be moving in three to four years, and you cannot afford to overpay for a home. We'll go through an example in a bit.

Let's look at how this normally plays out; I personally witness this happening at least a half dozen times a year. Buyer Bill wants to buy a home and asks real estate agent Sue to help him. After spending several days looking at properties, the buyer falls in love with a home that has an asking price of $220,000. He tells his agent that he would like to offer $210,000. However, the house has a fair market value of $200,000. (But the buyer is not aware of that yet. The real estate agent would have to run the "comps": the comparable properties similar to the house the buyer is interested in that have sold in that neighborhood in the past six months.) Here is where many agents go astray. Unfortunately, the answer many of them give the buyer is, "Great! Let me write that up for you and submit the offer to the seller." They know full well that the home isn't worth that and that the seller will likely jump on the offer or make a counteroffer very close to it. Either way, they're looking at an hour or two of paperwork, and few phone calls to coordinate inspections. Then thirty days later, the property closes and they get their commission check and they're off, never to be seen or heard from again.

Now what should have happened? A good, honest, reputable agent would have told the buyer, "First, before we make an offer, let me run the comps on the home to see how fairly or accurately it's priced ... Now based on the comps and the amenities the home has, I don't see that property being worth more than $200,000. If you want to try and get it at the fair market value, you need to offer $180,000 or $185,000, and see if they're willing to come down in price." The agent knows that an offer 20 percent below asking price rarely results in a sale, and that this offer-counteroffer-counter-counteroffer process will likely take several days, and in the end, the deal probably won't happen. They'll likely have to start all over again, spending even more days driving the buyer around town looking at another twenty or thirty houses. Whew! That is a lot of time and effort. If the agent had just kept his or her mouth shut, the $210,000 offer could have been submitted, the deal would have happened, and they would be done.

And now you can see why many agents take the route described above—less work and more money sooner. Finding that rare agent who is willing to sacrifice a commission check to prevent the client from paying too much for a home is absolutely critical to purchasing a home properly at or below market value.

So how do you find one of these agents? Realtor.com, Zillow, or any number of other real estate services and websites? Friends and family? When asked this question, many of our clients tell us they go to these sites and read the reviews of many of these agents. First of all, who is writing these reviews? That's right, clients just like you who know very little about real estate. Most of these reviews read the same: "Our agent was wonderful. She was very prompt in returning our calls and e-mails!" Okay, the agent was nice and friendly and courteous, but that doesn't mean they're a good real estate agent! Guess what? Most real estate agents are nice and friendly and courteous. That's part of their job; it's a service industry. What is most important is that agent's real estate acumen, how good is the agent in finding properties at or under market value. How accurate is his or her comparable figures and valuation computations? How deep is the agent's understanding of market trends, especially concerning growing/expanding parts of towns, neighborhoods, and so on? How expansive is the agent's understanding of the rental market and rental areas? These are the real estate traits you should be looking for. So how do you find these rare agents?

Fortunately for you, you don't need to because you now know me. I do know how to find these rare agents because I've been in the real estate industry for almost thirty years, and we've been helping our clients relocate around the country for over a decade. As a licensed broker, I know the intricacies of the real estate world, and I know the motivational forces that guide associates, brokers, and agency owners. Over the years we've refined a process of finding these agents, performing background checks and personal interviews with each and every one of them. At the end of this process, there is absolutely no misunderstanding between any of the parties. All actions taken will be for the sole purpose of meeting the clients' needs and financial best interests. If at any point I begin to question an agent's motivations, due diligence, and performance with respect to one of our clients, no client will ever be referred to that agent again.

There were a couple agents last year who received twelve clients from our referrals, with an average commission check of approximately $6,000, That's roughly $72,000 that we've handed those agents on a silver platter. Moreover, they didn't spend one penny on advertising or lead generation to get that business. It's business they got from doing their real estate profession extremely well with the highest of integrity and taking great care of our clients. Do you think either of those agents is going to risk losing our referrals just to make a quick buck on a deal? As far as they're concerned, we're the golden goose that keeps on giving. They're going to do everything in their power to ensure our clients get the best deals possible. Additionally, in contrast to every other agent-finder service out there, absolutely no agents can buy (pay a fee) their way into our network. Nor can they even solicit us to include them in our network. The only way for an agent to be included in our network across the country is for me to find them. We don't care who they work for—we've got Re/Max agents, Coldwell agents, Century 21 agents, local independent agents. It doesn't matter to us. We simply care that they are great real estate professionals, and that they take great care of our clients.

Notes

6

FSBOs/For Sale by Owner

THERE ARE NUMEROUS FSBO-TYPE BUSINESSES out there, as well as the standard homeowner who simply puts a "For Sale" sign in his or her yard. In many markets, this is especially prevalent during seller's markets, or when there is a high demand for housing and relatively low supply. They simply are trying to take advantage of the market conditions and get a high price for their home. There is absolutely nothing wrong with people trying to sell their own homes, but that doesn't mean you have to rush out there and buy one! Let's take a couple minutes and look at how a home normally gets listed by a real estate agent and put on the market for sale.

When somebody wishes to sell a property, he or she contacts a real estate agent (or interviews several agents) and ask for a current market analysis to inform the person approximately how much to list the house for. Agents accomplish this market analysis by looking at the comps for homes sold in the past six or twelve months in that neighborhood. By accessing the local MLS, they can get an average, low, and high price per square foot. Based on the seller's home square footage and the amenities, an approximate listing price (market value) is determined. If the seller decides to list the home with an agent, a listing agreement (contract) is drawn up that basically says the agent and agency will perform certain functions in advertising and promoting the sale of the home, and in return, the seller will pay 6 percent (typical amount but can be negotiated) of the sales price. If another agent brings a buyer who eventually buys the home, the seller's agent splits the 6 percent, giving the other agent 3 percent.

DAVID L. RUFFIN

Notice: Your agent receives the compensation from the seller, not you. Since you don't pay your buyer's agent any money, why in the would you ever not use an agent when buying a home?

With FSBOs, this process rarely happens. The seller normally sees other homes in the neighborhood sell and finds out through neighborhood gossip the price for which it sold. Invariably, all sellers think they have the nicest homes in the neighborhood, and it is at this point in the process when emotions take over. "Barbara sold her home for $250,000. I have coffee over there every Wednesday, and my home is much nicer than hers." *Bang*, asking price $275,000! No evidence, facts, math, science—nothing. Just pure emotion. Maybe Barbara's home was two hundred square feet larger. Maybe she sold it to an uninformed buyer who wrongly paid too much. The point is that no market-driven justifications go into a majority of FSBOs' asking prices.

Now I don't want you to think that all FSBOs are bad deals. We sell/buy about half a dozen a year, but we are involved throughout the process, providing our buying client with our real estate expertise, advice, and assistance. We tell our clients that if they happen to drive by a FSBO property that they are interested in, to simply call the number on the sign and ask the seller if they are willing to work with your buyer's agent (i.e., are they willing to pay your agent 3 percent of the selling price). Many sellers are more than willing to do that because they would still be saving a significant amount of money (3 percent). Once again, if you do not use an agent to represent you as the buyer, you don't have anybody to run the comps and tell you what the fair market value of the home is. You will be forced to simply take the seller's word for it. And since you are not paying your agent, why in the world wouldn't you want to take advantage of their expertise and advice.

Other than a strong seller's market, why do people try to sell their homes themselves? There are several reasons. Maybe they cannot afford to pay 6 percent to sell their home. Maybe they paid

REAL ESTATE 101

too much when they bought it themselves. Maybe their home has not appreciated in value enough for the time that they've lived there. Do not make the seller's financial problems your financial problems. It's usually best to just walk away. Sometimes deals just can't be done, not because of some deficiency in the property, but because of the financing underlying all of it.

As I alluded to earlier, many FSBOs will not have a problem working with and paying your buyer's agent. But occasionally, you'll find an FSBO who absolutely will not work with any agent. Don't walk away—run away as fast as you can! From my experience, there are usually only a few reasons why this might happen. One, their financial position is so tenuous they cannot even afford to pay 3 percent to your agent. Again, don't make the seller's financial problems your financial problems! Two, there is something going on with the home/property that they know a real estate professional will likely find—termites, structural issues, water damage, roof damage, and so on. When a buyer walks into a home, they look in all the rooms and imagine their stuff in that space. They look at the paint colors, tile and carpet, cabinets and appliances. While that is indeed important, real estate professionals walk through the house looking for the red flags mentioned previously—damage, deficiencies, big items that are going to be expensive to fix.

Another situation just makes me cringe. Not because the offer is so horrible, but because so many people fall for it. When an FSBO is trying to sell a home (say a $200,000 home), he or she tells the prospective buyer, "Hey, if we do this deal without the real estate agents, I'll save $12,000 in agent fees, and I'll split the savings with you. Otherwise, I'll have to increase the price of the house." First off, the home is worth what the home is worth—the market value regardless of the seller's expenses! Whether or not there are real estate agents involved is irrelevant to the value of the home. Second, and most important, I ask you to tell me how often in your entire life a complete stranger has come up to you and offered you thousands and thousands of dollars. It doesn't happen. If they tell you that they're going to split the savings with you, they're lying to you. We see family members try to take advantage of other family members when it comes to real estate deals, and it can get really ugly really fast. If you have an agent working on your behalf, it eliminates much of the uncertainty concerning price because your agent will show you the current comps for that home and neighborhood. You will then have the confidence that you bought the home for the right price, and you will therefore enjoy the home that much more, rather than worry the entire time you live there that you paid too much.

7

The VA Loan: Military Benefits for Home Ownership

IF YOU HAVE SERVED FOR a while, you're probably pretty familiar with the VA loan, or at least heard it mentioned around your unit. If not, a little background would probably help.

The Veterans Administration, or VA, helps servicemembers, veterans, and eligible surviving spouses become homeowners. They do this by providing a home loan guaranty benefit and other housing-related programs to help you buy, build, or repair a home for your personal occupancy. VA home loans are provided by private lenders such as banks and mortgage companies; the VA guarantees a portion of the purchase price, reducing the risk for the lender that should result in the lender providing you with more favorable terms. Lower interest rates compared to conventional, no mortgage insurance, and sometimes lower lender fees are offered. We highly recommend you consult a lending professional to guide you through the process.

There are several specific programs within the VA: purchase loans, cash-out refinance, interest rate reduction refinance loan (IRRRL), Native American direct loan (NADL), and adapted housing grants. With a purchase loan, the VA guarantees up to 25 percent of the purchase price in most situations, so you are not required to provide a down payment, avoid mortgage insurance, and receive interest rates unmatched by comparable conventional loan scenarios.

The VA's cash-out refinance loan is for homeowners who want to take cash out of their homes' equity to take care of concerns like paying off debt, funding school, or making home improvements.

The IRRRL, sometimes referred to as streamlined refinance, can help you lower your interest rate on your existing VA loan.

The NADL helps eligible Native American veterans finance the purchase, construction, or improvement of homes on Federal Trust Land.

Adapted Housing Grants help veterans with a permanent and total service-connected disabilities purchase or build an adapted home, or to modify an existing home to accommodate their disabilities.

The guarantee the VA provides allows lenders to offer you with more favorable terms, and there are numerous advantages to using a VA loan: no down payment as long as the sales price doesn't exceed the appraised value, no private mortgage insurance premium requirement, limits on closing costs (some of which may be paid by the seller), and the lender cannot charge you a penalty if you pay off the loan early. There are several misconceptions out there about using the VA loan, but please remember that you can use the VA loan more than once. There are no restrictions on whether or not you are a first-time home buyer, and VA loans can be assumable as long as the new buyer qualifies for the VA loan via the servicer according to guidelines of lender and the VA.

The first step, which you can work through with your VA-approved lender, is applying for and receiving your valid certificate of eligibility (COE). You must have suitable credit, sufficient income, and a COE to get a VA-guaranteed home loan. The home must be for your primary residence (it cannot used to purchase an investment property). They can be used to buy a home or a condominium unit in a VA-approved project (double-check this with your lender before making an offer), build a home, purchase and improve a home, improve a home by installing energy-related or energy-efficient improvements, or buy a manufactured home and/or lot (it can be more difficult to locate lenders offering this type of product).

One final note. There are loan limits depending on where the property is located. The VA does not set a cap on how much you can borrow to finance your home, but there are limits on the amount of liability VA can assume, or guarantee, which usually affects the amount of money an institution will lend you. The loan limits are the amount a qualified veteran with full entitlement may be able to borrow without making a down payment. Loan limits vary by county since the value of a house depends in part on its location. You can exceed the county loan limit by providing 25 percent of the difference between the purchase price and the county loan limit to make up the difference.

The basic entitlement available to each eligible veteran is $36,000. Lenders will generally loan up to four times a veteran's available entitlement without a down payment, provided the veteran is income- and credit-qualified and the property appraises for the asking price. Interest rates are subject to change due to market fluctuations. You can check the entitlement for your county by visiting the VA website.

Notes

8

Selling a Property

HOMEOWNERSHIP, BESIDES BEING PART OF the American dream, is one of the greatest moments in most people's lives. Besides marriage (tongue-in-cheek for some of you out there) and the births of your children, when you purchase a home, especially your first home, there is a great sense of achievement, security, and happiness. You very quickly forget about those wonderful aspects when orders arrive, and you now must face the challenges of having to move. And that starts with selling your current home.

For twenty years, I've tried to sell every one of the homes that I have lived in. For twenty years, I have failed to sell any of them by myself. And I have done it all, the sell it by owner programs, paid the reduced amounts to get it listed in the local MLS, advertised in the paper, internet; you name it, I tried it. I eventually sold all those homes—after I listed them with a real estate professional.

I will always be truthful with my clients, and in doing so, I sometimes reveal some of the dirty little secrets that most folks, especially other real estate agents, won't talk about. Why? Because I've been there. I've been a consumer, a sell it by owner, a real estate associate, and now a licensed broker. Most important, I'm a veteran, and that's more important than all the rest. So if I have the opportunity to point out a few tidbits here and there to help you make good decisions in the face of significant challenges, then I'm going to do so.

We've known several clients who have sold their own homes without a real estate agent. We honestly couldn't be happier for them, and it saved them thousands of dollars! When people come to us and ask our advice on selling their homes, we don't immediately jump into the listing sales pitch like 90 percent of the agents out there. You see, it may not be in the clients' best interests to list their homes with a real estate company. There's a shocking concept, the clients' best interests. They may have paid too much for the property years earlier and cannot afford to pay the professional fees and write a check at closing. They may currently live in a depressed market and didn't get the appreciation they expected. There are many factors involved, and when we see that is the case, we do everything we can to help them sell it themselves. Sometimes all we get is a percentage or two for helping them with the legal requirements and paperwork—and the satisfaction that a military family has successfully navigated a major part of their PCS and isn't hurt financially!

Our agents across the country, even though they may work for different real estate brokerages, share our beliefs and focus on the client. You are the reason Mil PCS, Inc. is in existence. You are the reason we do what we do.

Reduced Commissions

Ah, the reduced commission. One of my favorite topics. It never fails that when we get called to interview with a potential home seller that within the first few minutes, the potential client pulls out the *20 Questions You Must ask a Realtor* that they downloaded off the internet the night before. Question 2 or 3 is almost always, "Will you sell my house for a reduced commission?" Or, "What level of service will we receive for a particular commission rate?"

Don't get me wrong. You absolutely should interview any potential real estate agent. More important, you should interview your

REAL ESTATE 101

friends and coworkers. Get their recommendations. Interview the different real estate companies in the area. Interview the local real estate association for your city or town, and find out who the top sellers were. In fact, we do a lot of that for you. Before an agent can be part of our network, he or she is scrutinized by us. We developed our own checklist and interview that not only tells us the obvious public information but gives us a pretty good idea as to their honesty, integrity, and motivations. We only want agents willing to put the clients' interests above all else.

Now back to the checklists and interviews and reduced commissions. Here in our local town there are agents (and one in particular who is notorious for doing this) that offer to list homes for reduced commissions to say, "Thank you for your military service." Sounds good, doesn't it? Heck, 5 percent instead of 6 percent on a $200K home is a $2,000 savings! But here's the problem with those agents and those arrangements (dirty little secret). When they list your home in the MLS (cooperative listing service for all the agents in the area), it goes in as a 2.5 percent commission listing. The 5 percent you are paying is split between the listing agent and the selling agent. When another agent has a buyer in town looking to purchase a home, the buyer will ask their agent to print a list of available homes in a certain price range, square footage, and so on. So that agent compiles a list of possible homes to purchase and may come up with twenty-five homes. If twenty-two of those homes offer 3 percent and yours and two others offer 2.5 percent, where on that list of homes do you think your property is going to be listed? Yes, at the bottom. How hard is that selling agent going to push to sell their client a home that earns them half a percent less in commission? Not very. All other things being equal, homes listed at a reduced commission take longer to sell. If you have moved because you had orders and your house sits vacant for an extra month, there goes that 1 percent you were saving in an extra mortgage payment you shouldn't have had to make.

What irritates the heck out of me is that these agents offer reduced commissions purportedly out of their so-called kindness to say thank you, when more often than not, all they are trying to do is collect as many listings as they can, so they can sit back and let other agents sell their properties. Remember that notorious agent in our area? Believe it or not, she and her husband actually admitted that verbatim to me in some attempt to prove their business expertise.

Reduced commissions are great as long as you demand that your agent list it at full commission and that they take the full reduction themselves. That would be an honest, "Thank you."

Okay, you have decided to sell your house, and you have selected an agent. Now what? With the thousands of homes we have seen for sale, there are three things that almost always are must-do items. If your house is clean, updated, and decluttered, it will most likely sell. If it doesn't, you probably do not have it priced correctly. Obviously the above two sentences will not replace detailed market analysis, which you will get from one of our network agents. But if you asked us what three basic things are that an owner can do to help their house sell, that's it—clean, update, declutter!

The most important time of your property's listing life are the first ten to fourteen days. The first thing almost every agent in town does each morning is open up the local MLS and hit the button that says, "New Listings." They want to see what new properties are on the market. If it's a good one, they are going to rush their buyers out to see it before anybody else does. First impressions are critical. Again, if your house is not clean, updated, and decluttered, those agents will remember that particular house on so and so street isn't worth looking at. They'll remember that two weeks later, even if you've cleaned since then. Don't list your house until it's ready.

Clean

My goodness! You wouldn't believe the number of listings we go to where people are honestly expecting to sell the house, and it is absolutely filthy. Are you kidding me? Unless the buyer is looking for a fixer-upper and is going to try and steal the property with a lowball offer, this is an absolute showstopper. Clean your home. Hire somebody to clean your home. Don't list your home until it is clean.

Update

Okay, got to be a little careful here. It is not absolutely critical that you've got granite countertops, tile or hardwood floors, or custom mirrors installed throughout your home. Those are luxury items, and although they will help you get top dollar for your house, not having them will not necessarily prevent your house from selling. We're more concerned with a house that was obviously built and decorated twenty to thirty years ago. Wood paneling throughout, orange shag carpet, you know what we're talking about. When considering updating, consult your real estate professional (and read the next chapter). In a nutshell, bathrooms and kitchens normally provide the highest return on your investment.

Declutter

First and foremost, you want potential buyers to be able to picture your home as "their" home. They can't do that with all of your stuff everywhere. Okay, that was a little harsh, but you get my point. There's an entire industry that popped up specifically for this—the professional home stager. A few years ago, I hired a stager to help me sell my home on the East Coast. I "donated" almost $700 for her to tell me basically what I already knew. Remove as many furniture items from each room that you can without it looking funny or taking away functionality. You'll be surprised at how much cleaner and bigger the rooms look. Also remove the personal items and pictures. They want to visualize their wedding picture on the wall, and it is difficult to do that with an 18² × 22² framed picture of some strangers staring at them. We often suggest getting a little storage room or a Pods-type unit. Clients don't mind seeing that in the driveway because they know it will be leaving.

Any quality agent (all of our network agents) should absolutely tell you the things you need to do to sell your home. You're hiring them to do just that, not to be your friend. Insist that they be critical. Anything less will end up costing you more money.

Notes

9

Updating a Property

AS THE PREVIOUS CHAPTER MENTIONED, updating your home can be a crucial step in the successful listing and selling of your property. It is not always the determining factor, but as active real estate agents, we've seen and heard hundreds of comments about properties that are outdated, and almost all of them are negative. Occasionally we'll run across that savvy buyer who can truly overlook old, dated furnishings and amenities to see the future possibilities and hidden value, but they are few and far between. Most often, it simply leaves a negative impression on the potential buyer.

So how do you determine what to update and what to leave alone? Ask! Ask your friends who just sold their home. Ask a design professional in a furniture store. Ask other real estate professionals you may know. Ask us! But most important, ask the network agent we put you in touch with. One of the reasons we've included agents in our network is their expertise in all facets of real estate, including how to stage a home properly. There are several factors that will go into this decision, and we'll cover them in the next few paragraphs.

To see how this all works, let's look at some basic examples and numbers. Say you purchased your 2,000 square foot home five years ago for $200,000, you paid $100 per square foot. Now that it is time to sell, one of our network agents will provide you with a market analysis (the comps) to give you an idea of the current value of your home. You'll definitively want to pay attention to this because that is exactly what any potential buyers and their agents will be doing.

A real estate agent's market analysis will highlight comps for all similar homes that have sold in your area in the past six to twelve months. They show the high, low, and average prices per square feet. A home that is in great condition and fully updated will be comp'd at the high rate, and one that is run-down and not updated at all will be at the low rate. And for most of us, we are usually somewhere in between. Using our example, if the high for your area is $105/square foot, that means at most you're likely to sell for $210,000, and it wouldn't make any sense to invest $15,000 or $20,000 in upgrades since the market likely won't support that high of a price. Now let's say the neighborhood has appreciated nicely, and the high comps are $120/square foot. That would mean a $20,000 upgrade investment might garner a $240,000 selling price, and that would be a solid investment.

Now that you have an idea of how the system works, it is time for you to determine what items you would like to improve and how much money you should invest in doing so. Sometimes the best answer, practically and financially, may simply be cosmetic (paint, cleaning, and so on) changes. Other times it may mean anything from swapping out appliances to major remodeling. Exploring all the possibilities could fill numerous articles. We'll do our best to summarize.

Starting

So you've decided to do some home improvements. Now where do you start?

First and foremost is the financial feasibility. It doesn't do you any good to invest $30,000 in a complete kitchen and bath remodel if it will only net you and extra $10,000 on the selling price. Historically, kitchens and bathrooms offer the highest returns on your investments. Investing $10,000 on new kitchen countertops will go much farther than $10,000 worth of landscaping in the backyard.

We suggest using a conservative approach to figuring your upgrade budget. We do not recommend targeting the high price per square foot. If you end up getting it, great! Just don't assume you will. There are too many other factors and variables that will affect how soon you will sell your house and for what price. Using our $200,000 purchase example, a high comp would value your house at $240,000. I recommend using approximately $225,000 as a target price, giving you a $15,000 potential upside and greater flexibility to negotiate selling price and cover professional fees.

We recommend approaching this project this way.

> $200,000 purchase price
> $13,500 professional fees (6 percent commission on $225,000)
> <u>$3,500 closing costs</u>
> $217,000 breakeven

After discussion with your real estate agent, you determine that $4,000 in paint and flooring would easily justify $113 per square foot, giving you a target price of $226,000. If you sold the house for that price, you would make a nice profit of about $5,000. Another option would be a more extensive plan, say one requiring $15,000 in upgrades, which may yield $117 per square foot for a target price of $234,000. Under this scenario, your profit would only be $2,000! Although this is a hypothetical situation, we have seen this play out for real many times. You absolutely need to sit down with one of our network agents and work through this. More is not always better.

Another component is when to do the work and who to do it. There's a lot to be said about sweat equity. Performing the work yourself can save you thousands. For example, replacing a laminate floor with ceramic tile is a great upgrade. But in most parts of the country, you can figure on the labor being three times the cost of the product (a $2,000 job being $500 of materials, $1,500 in labor).

Most home improvement stores, like Lowe's and Home Depot, offer free classes on how to do many home projects. So installing a $2,000 floor for $500 in materials and a little hard work can be a great upgrade and give you quite a bang for your buck! Likewise, paint can be a great upgrade. Not only does everything look better, but the smell gives the potential buyer a strong impression of an updated home. But be forewarned: A bad paint job is worse than no painting at all, so take your time and do it well.

In summary, pencil out the finances to start organizing your planning. We've all heard horror stories of $10,000 projects that ended up costing $20,000! Also, work closely with your network real estate agent to determine the best possible asking price that will get you the quickest sale for the most money. If your asking price is too high, each month that passes without your home selling costs you even more.

Project Decisions

First, a point of caution. Although we are big proponents of sweat equity, certain jobs require professionals. As a general rule of thumb, if the project demands a trade skill that normally requires a license or certification—such as electrical, plumbing, HVAC, or structural—it is normally best to hire professionals. Obviously, we're talking about more extensive work than just changing a light switch cover or toilet float. If you try to do the extensive rework yourself, you'll likely end up hiring a professional later to fix your screwups, thus eliminating any money you may have saved.

So what kind of projects should you focus on? As I mentioned previously, kitchens and bathrooms historically offer the highest returns on your investments, so we usually advise clients to look there first. Also, remodels that increase square footage increase the value of your home, so finishing a basement or attic space

REAL ESTATE 101

could add significant value to your property. As we alluded to earlier, all upgrades are not created equally. Investing $10,000 on new kitchen countertops will go much farther than $10,000 worth of landscaping in the backyard.

Kitchen and bathroom upgrades don't necessarily have to cost a small fortune. Old, worn-out cabinets can absolutely be transformed by being sanded down, repainted or stained, and new hardware installed. We recently remodeled an entire kitchen for less than $1,300 ($700 tile floor, refinished cabinets for $75 in sandpaper and hardware, $400 oven/stove, $75 paint). That new kitchen yielded us over $10,000 in profit on that investment.

Bathrooms are often overlooked but can be critical to a home selling. Back when your author was young and single, he bought a house that was absolutely perfect for him. Unfortunately it was far from perfect for most of the potential buyers because the master bath was extremely small. Increasing the size of the bathroom would have been impossible, or at least very expensive, having to build new walls, move plumbing, and so on. Instead, we replaced the old, bulky vanity with a very stylish pedestal sink and changed the flooring, shower hardware, and mirrors. It wasn't perfect, but for about $500, it was no longer a negative when showing the house.

Landscaping is a much discussed and somewhat controversial upgrade. Most real estate professionals will tell you that there is very little return on investment when it comes to landscaping. However, curb appeal is very real. It doesn't do any good to have the greatest kitchen in the world if no potential buyer ever gets past the front yard to see it! Hiring professionals will cost a significant amount, but doing it yourself can save a lot of money and yield tremendous benefits. Don't worry about not having any design talent. Drive around your neighborhood, look at the other homes with landscaping you like, and take ideas from several of them. Be creative, and you'd be amazed at what you'll come up with. Another great benefit from this technique is that your landscaping won't be out of place for the neighborhood.

Most important, discuss your improvement ideas with your network real estate agent. That's what they are paid to do! They see hundreds of homes every month and talk to buyers and sellers constantly. They have the experience, expertise, and insight that will assist you in making the very best decisions you can.

And don't forget to save all your receipts. Most home repairs and improvements for the purpose of selling your house is a tax deduction (talk to your CPA). Good luck with your projects.

Notes

10

The Purchase Process

ALL RIGHT, IT'S TIME TO find and purchase your home. Where do you start?

Step 1: Get prequalified. Call your lender (we can help you with that selection as well), and tell them that you would like to get "pre-qual'd" to buy a home. The lender will do a soft credit check and compute a simple debt-to-income ratio. In order for them to do this, they'll need your gross income from all sources and your long-term liabilities (student loans, car loans, significant credit card debt, and so on). It's important to use the figures for the proper time and place. If you're a 2LT currently at Vance AFB in Enid, Oklahoma, and you've received orders to Charleston AFB, South Carolina, and you pin on 1LT next month, use your O-2 pay with Charleston BAH since that is what you'll be at the time of home purchase.

Usually at this point, you don't have a specific house in mind, so you're just getting a general idea how much of a mortgage you can qualify for. The numbers vary by lending institution and time, but generally speaking, with good credit, lenders will loan up to approximately 47 percent for a conventional loan and slightly higher for a VA loan. For example, you have $5,000 gross monthly income and $1,400 in total loan payments. That gives you $3,600 available; 47 percent of which is about $1,700, and that equates to a monthly payment on a $250,000 to $275,000 home. Don't worry about figuring all this out on your own. Your lender has computer programs that do all of this very quickly. What's important is that now you know you're prequalified to $265,000, and you can give that to your real estate agent to assist in searching for the right home for you. It would be a waste of time to look at $300,000 homes if you're only qualified to $250,000.

One final note on your pre-qual. This number is not set in stone; it's just a basic guideline. If you're prequalified to $250,000 and fall in love with a home for $260,000 or $265,000, just call your lender, and most likely you'll be just fine. Once you get a home under contract, then you'll do the formal mortgage application and start the actual loan approval.

Note: We recommend working with the lender to get preapproved rather than just prequalified. For most active-duty members, the only difference is providing 1 month's bank statements, most recent LES, and the most recent year's W-2(s). Preapproval is slightly more extensive, but these are things you'll be required to provide for the actual loan approval anyway. It is best to ensure you have taken the approval process as far as it can go to show the listing agent and the seller that you have provided all necessary documents thus far, and an underwriter has approved the loan rather than just the automated underwriting system.

Step 2: Now that you know generally how much home you can afford, tell your agent to send you the listings at least a week before you plan on going on your house-hunting trip. Note that in competitive markets, this may not be possible due to short time frames on the market and multiple offer situations. You may want to shorten the period to two or three days prior. Give your agent some general parameters: $250,000, three bedrooms with an office or four bedrooms, fenced backyard, three-car garage, and so on. Setting these basic parameters is important, or you'll end up with more than a hundred listings to go through. After thirty or forty, they all start to look the same, and it becomes far too time-consuming. Your agent will then send the listings to you (or a link to the listings), and out of those thirty or forty, you'll need to pick out the top fifteen to twenty that you actually want to look at in person and see first-hand. Make sure you send those listings you picked out to your agent at least a couple days before you plan on being there. They'll need time to set up the showings with the seller's agent.

Step 3: Now it's time to look at the properties. Depending on how much time you spend in each home, you can probably plan on seeing eight to ten homes per day. Take some general notes; by the time you get to home number 17, you've probably forgotten what houses one, two, and three looked like. Once you've finished the homes, it's not unusual to go back and look again at your top three or four choices. Once you've got your top choices, don't forget to ask your agent to run the comps for those properties. It is the only way to gauge the approximate fair-market value. Also, you may want to check on HOA (homeowners' association) dues, property taxes, and insurance as these factors will directly affect your total monthly mortgage payment.

Step 4: It is now time to make an offer. Keep in mind that the price isn't the only negotiable item. Do you want them to leave the washer and dryer? Do you want the seller to pay some or all of your closing costs? Do you want the seller to buy you a one-year home warranty or to close in sixty days instead of thirty days? Speak with your agent about all these items. In most states, in order for an offer to be a legitimate, legal contractual offer, it must be accompanied by something a value, or "earnest money," usually in the form of a check. This earnest money shows the seller that you are a serious buyer and also protects the seller from you simply changing your mind three weeks later and walking away from the deal. When a property is under contract (the buyer and seller have agreed on the price and terms and both have signed all the necessary documents), that home is taken off the market. If you were simply to walk away from the deal, the seller would be harmed at not having the past three weeks to sell the home to somebody else. In that circumstance, the seller would keep your earnest money. Your earnest money check will usually be cashed and deposited in an escrow account in your name and be applied to your closing costs or the price of the home. In other words, the check you write for your earnest money is *your* money and will be used on *your* behalf. The only way you typically lose your earnest money is if you change your mind and walk away for no legitimate reason.

Step 5: Once the home is under contract, there now becomes a lot of moving pieces to the process. Specifically for you as the buyer, your lender will require that you start the formal loan application and provide them with a lot of documents. These typically include two years of tax returns, two months of bank statements, two months of LESs, and proof of service statement (for VA loans). Get these documents to your lender as soon as possible so that you are not the reason your loan is delayed.

While you are doing this, your agent is arranging to have the property inspected. Always get a home inspection. It will be the best $300 to $500 you spend. Whether or not you get a whole home inspection or individual inspectors, that is up to you. Ask your agent for his or her recommendation. Agents typically know who the good, reputable inspectors are. Regardless of which method you choose, you need at the very least electrical and plumbing inspections and possibly roof and structural inspections if any deficiencies are apparent.

Step 6: Based on the inspection results, you as the buyer will submit a TRR (treatments, repairs, requirements) to the seller asking them to repair certain items. Be somewhat judicious about what you ask for. Your inspection report will likely have thirty or forty items noted, but only a handful of them will be important or expensive. You want the seller to pay for these items! If you submit a TRR with every little problem (broken light bulb), they'll agree to fix the little things but not the major items. The TRR is typically a negotiating point in the process. Please note that if you are not satisfied with the inspection results, you can at this point usually back out of the deal, and you will get your earnest money back. Once the buyer and seller agree on the repairs, you both sign the final TRR, and the process moves forward.

Step 7: Once you've had the inspections and signed the TRR, you are basically done until closing. Your lender, however, has probably ordered the appraisal; you pay for it, but the lender orders it. Once your lender has the appraisal, they package it with all of your documents and send it to the underwriters, who give the lender the final approval to lend you a specific amount of money to purchase a specific property. When your lender has that approval from the underwriters, they will let your agent and title/closing company know that you have approval to close. The very last step is that your closing company will send you your closing documents (closing disclosure) approximately four days before closing. It details the exact amounts that all parties will be spending or receiving at closing.

Expected Fees

Many clients, both past and present, are confused about what fees the seller pays and what fees the buyer pays. If you're one of them, don't feel bad. These fees differ significantly according to the local market and different lenders. Many of these fees can also be negotiated and sometimes eliminated. After all, mortgage lenders are in a competitive business.

Below you will find a brief explanation of these costs. It may not include all items required specific to your property or the area in which you have purchased. This is a guide only. You'll want to discuss them with your agent or closing company.

Fees can range from 1 percent to 6 percent of total purchase price, excluding down payment.

Buyer's Fees

It's important to remember that this is just a general list. States have different rules, laws, and tax structures. And your lender and title/closing company also have some discretion on what your fees will be. Generally, the buyer's fees will include:

>Inspection Fees—General
>Inspection Fees—Detailed (roof, mold, asbestos, water damage, and so on)
>Mortgage Application and Appraisal—may be waived by bank
>Mortgage Insurance—may be added to the mortgage
>Legal Fees and Disbursements—due at closing
>Home Insurance—can be escrowed
>Moving and Storage expense
>Land Transfer tax/stamps
>Title Insurance
>Survey—new or updated

Seller's Fees

>Costs can range from 1.5 percent to 5 percent of total sale price.
>Real Estate Commissions
>Tax Proration
>Unpaid Homeowners' Fees
>Legal Fees and Disbursements—due at closing
>Survey—new or updated
>Mortgage Interest Adjustments—if applicable
>Moving and Storage expense

Step 8: Finally, it's time for the closing. Make sure you check with the closing company as to what type of funds you'll need to bring. It could be a personal check or certified funds. It may be best to wire the money the day before. Caution: Please do not wire any money to title/escrow without calling to confirm wiring instructions over the phone. Make sure to use a verified phone number, not one obtained from the e-mail with the wiring instructions. If one party's e-mail is hacked, you could become a victim of wire fraud, a growing trend in the industry.

With that taken care of, all you need to do now is show up at the closing office, sign your name a million times, and when you're done, they hand you keys to your new home. Congrats!

Notes

11

The Home Inspection

A CRITICAL PART OF THE purchase process is the home inspection. Generally, once you have a home under contract, it is time to schedule a home inspection. Based on the inspection results, you will have an idea of what repairs to ask the seller to make. These repairs are listed on the TRR. and will be submitted by your real estate agent to the seller.

When choosing inspections, you'll likely have the option of (1) getting a whole home inspector, or (2) getting individual inspectors (electrician, plumber, roofer, structural, and so on). There are pros and cons to both. Dave Clinton, founder of Capstone Home Inspections, provided a list of some key items to keep in mind:

- Whatever you think you know about properties and houses, a quality home inspector will know more. In many states, home inspectors are licensed and typically required to maintain continuing education to stay abreast of the latest industry items, regulations, and codes.

- Whole home inspections will cover many more systems on the home than if you just hired a roofer, electrician, and plumber. Home inspections will check foundations, visible framing, insulation, appliances, ducting, windows, doors, everything that is visible.

- Home inspectors will not be the ones accomplishing the repairs; therefore, they have no personal monetary incentive to making things sound worse than they really are. Individual inspectors may have more expertise when it comes to complex electrical or plumbing issues, but they may be guilty of inflating the inspection report because they know the seller will likely hire them to perform the repairs.

- A home inspection allows you to have a contingency clause in your contract stating the contract can be voided based on the inspection results or used for renegotiation.

- A whole home inspector will not only tell you what major problems exist in the home right now, but will provide a lengthy report that will also include items approaching the end of their service life, items that will need maintenance in the near future, and areas where normal maintenance might have been neglected. This will help you budget for maintenance and repairs, and give you an idea what it will cost to own the home over the next three to five years.

- A quality report will also help you learn about your home. It will tell you where the water and gas shut-off valves are, where the electrical shut-off location is and how to use it, where your plumbing cleanout location is, and the model and serial numbers for your major appliances in case repairs or parts are needed. If anything about the home is odd or something is located in an unusual place, it will be noted on the report. A quality report will help you learn and operate your home.

- You must prepare yourself for the report, however, because they can be overwhelming. It will seem like everything needs work. Being a home inspector is a high-liability business; as such, most inspectors identify every flaw possible to prove their attention to detail and to protect themselves from claims of negligence and liability. Clients

REAL ESTATE 101

must keep in mind that the inspector is not just writing up things that are broken or inoperative but anything that is not optimum. Even with a very good home, it can be extensive. For this reason, it is very beneficial for the client to be at the inspection or, as a minimum, be there at the end of the inspection to allow the inspector to verbally explain their findings and prepare their client for the report. If you are out of town or unable to attend, a good inspector will have no problem walking through the report with you over the phone. Either way, you will feel a lot better about the inspection after talking to him or her.

- When it comes to hiring the right inspector, like any profession, there are trustworthy and not so trustworthy individuals. It is not recommended that you hire the only inspector your realtor recommends. Do your homework and check around. There are many aids now available, such as Homeadvisor.com, and Angieslist.com. While these can be helpful, they are not foolproof methods. Sometimes, depending on the community, word of mouth might still be the best way. Keep in mind these websites charge the contractor for their services, and if that contractor has plenty of business without them, they might choose not to pay to be listed on that site. Also, be careful not to be overly impressed with national professional associations, societies, and so on. While they do provide some level of credibility, they do not guarantee a professional work ethic. Many simply require inspectors to pay an annual fee and show proof that they are licensed. In most states, home inspectors are required to renew their state licenses annually, which also requires annual continuing education to keep refreshing their professional knowledge.

- Keep in mind that sometimes realtors and home inspectors can have a bit of a strained relationship. Realtors are afraid of losing the sale based on the inspection and, as a result, may not prefer some inspectors. Take their recommendations, but call other home inspectors, talk to them (think interview), ask them questions—length of experience, experience before they were inspectors, the type of report they offer, and so on. Is the report tailored to the home or a check-the-box if it's broken type? In the end, your choice should come down to experience and reputation (customer reviews).

- Inspectors who do not want you at the home should send warning signals. You are the client, and they work for you. You should be encouraged to be there.

- This is not a time to worry about the cost of an inspection. By all means, call around and get some quotes. Most bids are usually within $150 to $200 of each other. You need to ask yourself if $150 is a concern when you're making a $200,000 investment. Sometimes it is still true that you get what you pay for.

- Don't leave choosing your home inspector to the last minute. A reputable home inspector could be completely booked for the next two to three weeks during busy times of the year. As soon as you sign a purchase agreement, the home inspector should be scheduled to ensure the inspection gets done in the required time.

- Remember that the inspector works for you, and the report is proprietary; the client owns the report. If you want it sent to your realtor or to the seller's realtor, it should be with your knowledge and consent.

Notes

12

Conclusion

I HOPE YOU HAVE FOUND this publication insightful and useful. This booklet is not intended to cover every aspect of a real estate transaction; it is intended to provide you a basic foundation to consider beginning your real estate life. Hopefully it has provided you with some fundamentals to real estate and will get you started with the right professionals and asking the right questions.

As I mentioned earlier, there are never any guarantees in life, especially when it comes to investing. There are inherent risks in any investment, whether it's stocks, bonds, mutual funds, or real estate. Our intent is to always minimize or mitigate as much of that risk as possible, because you can never eliminate it completely.

Work with true professionals, minimize risk, capitalize on opportunity, and weigh your options truthfully and honestly. The world of real estate can be a wonderful opportunity and I wish you all the very best!

Notes

www.ingramcontent.com/pod-product-compliance
Lightning Source LLC
Chambersburg PA
CBHW021309240526
45463CB00018B/892